THE BONEYARD, THE BIRTH MANUAL, A BURIAL: INVESTIGATIONS INTO THE HEARTLAND

Julia Madsen

The Boneyard, The Birth Manual, A Burial:
Investigations Into The Heartland by Julia Madsen
Published by Trembling Pillow Press
New Orleans, LA
ISBN-13: 978-1-7323647-0-7
Copyright © 2018 Julia Madsen

Typesetting and Design: Megan Burns
Cover Design: JS Makkos
Cover Art: Julia Madsen
Copyedit: Kia Alice Groom

NEW ORLEANS

THE BONEYARD, THE BIRTH MANUAL, A BURIAL: INVESTIGATIONS INTO THE HEARTLAND

Table of Contents
ಬಲ

For Tim and Angie

For one who sets himself to look at all earnestly, at all in purpose toward truth, into the living eyes of a human life: what is it he there beholds that so freezes and abashes his ambitious heart?

–James Agee, *Let Us Now Praise Famous Men*

I. THE BONEYARD

Before you drifted into midsummer's heat and static like a slow fog, the sumac unfurled, a string of days unending. In the lowlands sleep is like an irradiated small road, a refrain. Where days proceed chain-link or barbed wire, headlights shine through trees in the heat of night. An outline of branches.

Here the night. Hear transmissions. The wind writes your name in black lace, persimmon flowers cripple. You are like black wind now, growing more and more fervid. Blinking then gone.

Lurch of distance. Cattle settle into fields,

fattening with oats.

O blood outline,
branches pressed against a no-name landscape

cinched with silence.

Black lace billows and fades into a subliminal horizon. The sun blinks and goes blind. What are these images that waver just above our heads, melting?

In another dream your tongue swells and becomes thick like a slab in wind in the boneyard of whose longing wears a necklace of teeth.

The boneyard rattles with static, barbed wire, lightning.
Absence blowing over absence, the face of the desert.
In rain. Imagine. You didn't think you'd come back.
The hounds shudder. The screen door ajar.

In a fog of sumac, sweet and vague, the mirror, the screen door, a stutter. Hear that longing, an echo. Just west ago. On the edge of town the butcher sleeps alone in blind premonition.

You electric, you void, you stultify silence. You trace the way of unconscious arteries, crush tomatoes in your hands. Make a fist. Sit on the porch. You, sweating distance, listen   as the wind comes in to part the curtains.

The sidereal shields us like an arras, pulls into focus or tosses a sidelong glance. As if the thread of light under the curtains leans into. The vacancy of dreams. Or, a catalogue of things that follows from looking: empty parking lots, fruit stands, dead cattle, spoiled watermelon.

Is it true that rust fills these rooms

with the corpuscles of time.

It's fleeting.

Does the wind blow nothing in

when the hunter's gunshot echoes.

When the hunter's gunshot echoes, the landscape turns into smoke. Under the sleeve where the heart might be cuffed, birds fly out. Here magic is the stumbling block toward making sense feel enough to even tunnel the dark.

No. Magic is a no-name bar where dim lips press against drinking glasses in blind premonition. Dreamy or vague, the vacant smile, a promise of teeth, smoke blowing through neon green light spilling onto concrete. You don't leave. You never left.

Thoughts occur in multiples like double vision. Lightning strikes twice where no one could visit or light a cigarette. Do you feel the edges begin to feather, a soft vignette, the horizon slowly pulling into focus.

II. THE BIRTH MANUAL

Before the book began, the pages of the birth manual blew open in wind, birds flew out of the sleeves of books. There was rust and persimmon flowers. Dark rooms like membranes pulsating, detached, gray matter bleeding into other rooms. Snapshots into memories just on the border of then. Before the wound made legible, a function of ink and time.

The birth manual carries dust and genuflection, it is a loose binding of smudged and yellowed pages you once discovered as a child, buried. Deep under so many years of dirt and sleep and straw in the hayloft of a barn the color of rust. Whose vacant windows gazed onto. And there were reflections framed in windowpanes trapping light. There was wild oat and ragweed. Sweet clover, you were missing teeth. You pulled them out one by one with string. Bruised knees and you buried the yellowed pages in terrycloth like a trove or fine tincture the color of secrets running backwards in time's amnesia.

The birth manual's putrefaction is a compendium of collapse, an arbiter of glances hinting the bygone. And you came back for it. You never left. This is the first step.

This is the first step: the manual falls open in your lap. Peel away the spider webs laced between pages. Remember that this is also a book of occasions, one of them sleep. In the second step you fall asleep. Slowly where the wind streams in like a dream of installments, images stack against one another like slabs and in this dream you say *oo* and *aah* like a child, you speak like a child, you look upon that other world luminous in shadow, calculate its depth, it is an alphabet without sound but there is breath within it and powers, powers that take you into the blue light of premonition.

Into the blue light of premonition where the Sybil sits under the sign of BEWARE OF DOG, licking her wounds through absence you mark an X for wound or womb where absence should be.

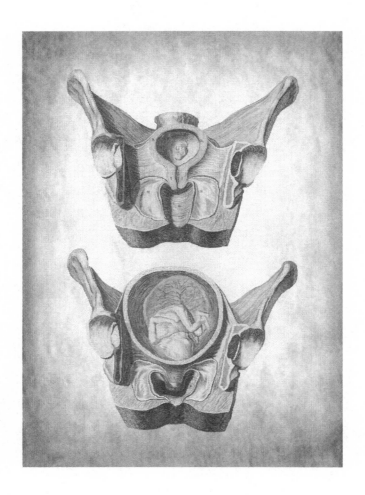

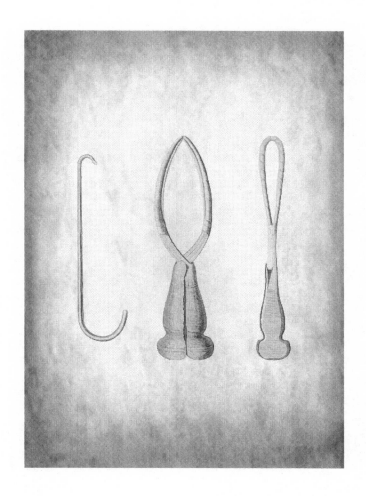

drop of Seed, nay only a fo
impregnate, and form a Child
tity of the Seed is finall, the fi
and weaker for it, or if the Ma
eafed, or the Womb ftuft with

nan, which injection could not
were firft moved ; neither coa
d but by frication of the parts,

ith a clean and bright needle a
ve conceived, the needle wit
l fpeckles, but if not, it will be

bleed but upon neceffity, fome
eeding but once, a little too
1 away, tho' others I confefs,
en times whilft they were with
    mifcarried.   Now feeling all
itution, they muft not be all
have moft blood can beft bear

If Purging be thought nece
be only ufed, as *Manna*,

Clytoris, from a Greek word, oufly to grope the privities. D in fhape, fituation, fubftance, and erection, and differs from bignefs : in fome it grows to t out from betwixt the lips of tl

the woman,during her month
s the company of her husband,
purged and void ; or elfe wher
great defire and luft with her
conceived ; or when fhe hath
courfes beyond her time.

How magic occurs in silence, alone, when nobody's around for miles and miles and you think now of small animals tunneling the dark. Think the fur of words stuck in anybody's teeth. Is this the butcher's secret, knowing what the farmer cannot speak? Is this the cattle of days following chain-link and tedious? Here where we are forever pulling rope, imagination takes over. If it didn't you'd be dead, the butcher imagines. The farmer swoons back. Blackbirds coo in the faraway.

Or, an imprint left by doubt, which now speaks from the faraway, within it, hold out your hands. An outline of fingers like branches. Press your hand against the page. Imagine a man in the desert spinning plates. Next, a woman wriggling inside a cocoon. And soon you begin to remember, but vaguely, a rose-tree almost vanishing.

III. A BURIAL

The glisten of dew, perfume of persimmon flowers, an X to mark the mound below the sign of BEWARE OF DOG. Morning wipes away the night's loose ends, the dog chain rattles. Home is womb bleeding all the way through, motherland, purged and voided beyond her time, so you keep the lights on in the morning at night, turn words around in your mouth until they form something more, unknowing, like why, for instance, time should exist here in the present-pastness of the pastoral where childhood's acres have all gone to smoke, even the old farmhouse burned down, and why should you find yourself here now, in the desert of the heartland, dragging the ghost of the real behind it.

The heartland is the desert of the real and if you can't imagine this then you're already on the gravel road traveling back toward fire and abandon. Dream-installments issue one after the next after the next in rapid succession, an animal hide shot through with holes touches the sky, a bird falls through fog, silent, where wood burns. Sweet clover, do you remember falling like a cadaver through air. *Cadere*. Would you remember running the acres, anywhere to turn to. But it wasn't you.   In snapshots approaching fog you begin to remember now: a handprint the color of rust. The outline of branches.

Walk back into memory's absence:
an outline of branches in the boneyard.
Where the butcher buries weight
and ash. A chain-link fence leading us
there. Forever. Did you see the misdeed
or just after, would you have seen
the rotten teeth of the guard dog
shuddering through all of this.

Neon green light, when you bite down on a pillow. In a halo of pilled blankets. Forever feels like that, sometimes, when sleep doesn't come it doesn't does it.

If it's true: then say it: we have always been alone. Here isolation translates all that goes unspoken. We slice off our words, chew the last bits or swallow them whole. Separate chaff from more chaff. Suck on lemongrass to spread the hours.

That which is brought out to the light the real light like a child.

Isolation is here to pick our pockets. There are birds on the wire. Take notes.

Winter's bad omen always comes to balance its books. In January amongst the living the snow fell harder, unrelenting, covering the landscape in white icy breath. Everyone kept under wraps. Even the meat packing factory closed its doors, this time for good.

When the factory shut down,

everybody knew. Without saying. It was only a matter

of time. *Some of us would be handed*

over. To time. Others knew

the factory's unconscious arteries

like the back of their hand:

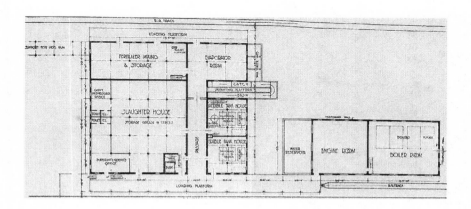

And maybe we knew then that the body was like a factory, out of steam and rundown, sputtering, on hinges. One man even cut off his penis. Some left wives and children in winter's rotten carcass shot through with light.

*The chain went so fast that it didn't give the animals
enough time to die.
I hung live birds on the line.
After a time, you see what happens.*

"One cut! One cut! One cut for the skin;
one cut for the meat."
The line was so fast there was no time to sharpen.
The knife gets dull and you have to cut harder.
That's when it really starts to hurt,
that's when you cut yourself.

*Two or three times a year I got infections
under my fingernails.
When I went to the clinic they froze my fingertips
and cut out the pus.*

"I don't see any blood, so I can't send you to a doctor."
She didn't write anything down,
she just told me to go back to knife sharp.

I pulled ribs with my fingers on the packing ribs line.
My fingers and nails were in constant pain
because the company wouldn't give us hooks
to pull the ribs, and they wouldn't let us bring our own.
They said that meat gets lost using hooks,
and using fingers pulls more meat.

They loved you if you were healthy and you worked like a dog, but if you got hurt you were trash. They will look for a way to get rid of you.

There's a lot of macho too.
The young guys especially didn't like to admit
they got hurt. They wanted to show that they're tough
so they kept working.
They didn't want to get teased.

*I was afraid to miss work to recover
because they would fire me for absenteeism.
I have to work to support my three children.*

Had the hunter not found himself without a job. Had he not taken work with the farmer hauling crop into the granary before spring. It was late February and the hounds were barking at nothing. They nipped at air. At the no-name bar on the corner everyone said the hunter had gone mad. The farmer didn't pay him. The hunter was out to balance the books.

What the hunter burrows in secret is a wish for decay, what hunger borrows. To pilfer in the name of (retribution by another name) (and never as sweet). The persimmon flowers fold in, hasp for leaves. Curtains close at the absence of a child. Void or missive. Missing. To do such a thing he couldn't, and did.

When one speaks of uncertainty here, they mean it. The blackbirds lift off, if not for the frightening angle, a shot in the dark. When everyone said the baby must have crawled off. Into snow. Somehow and yet. The fog lights darkened when the hunter took that bundle of cloth and buried it in the boneyard, just under a rose-tree, almost vanishing. Had the butcher and his dog not been asleep.

They will look for a way to get rid of you.

Between now and then you turn back.
Memories of mothers follow
propped open like the pages of a book
to take care of all this flesh and weight,
ready and primed for the bloodier parts.

The fact that we get so little and need so much.

My mother got married
and she didn't finish high school,
and she sure wanted me to finish.
She didn't want me to end up like her
in this small town. Like I am now.

Can't afford tires for our truck.
They keep going flat…
School trips, pictures, any school functions,
or anything that my kids just want,
I just can't get it.
I just cannot do it.

I just wish there was no such thing as money to an extent.
'Cause it hurts my kids, it hurts our family.
Can't always get what you want, and I know that,
but it's just hard sometimes.

My mom, grandmother, great grandma all said
make sure you have enough
because you want to eat,
and if you have extra, you save.

*I'm the only one working right now
and we can't really save anything.*

The most important thing is our truck.
We have to have it. So we try to save as much
as we can for that payment.
And if we don't pay it, they will come get it.

I worry about the kids' future,
especially with the economy the way it is right now,
with my husband being laid off.

Everything is a need right now.
Like right now,
she's outgrown all of her clothes
and we have to buy diapers every month.

And you know money gets tight.
I think everybody, almost everybody's
probably living paycheck to paycheck
nowadays anyways.

It's just a matter of how good you get at it—as to how well you survive.

If we say, it is true that the young here are flung into motherhood, if we intimate that the birth manual cannot prepare one for survival. Only ritual. Of doubt. Without saying it. How do we say, a child is being killed. And know what is meant. In our dark hearts. Abandoned to winter.

You ran the acres as though you could run away, you thought you could get so far.

You weren't so far off.
You never left.
And ran and ran for days.

Have we learned to brace ourselves
for what goes unremitted at remote
angles: a trace in snow
that fades by morning.

Have lingered for days
in fields flattened into focus.

The lenses freeze over,
laced with crystalline patterns
holding up a mirror to time
to reflect the past and future tense,
but what do we have now
to show for it.

Were you to come back, were you to have never left, you might find yourself pulling sumac, lighting a cigarette in the foggy afterhours. Might find yourself on the outskirts of town where the butcher lives alone. He could stand for all that has not been shut down or boarded up.

To place abandoned to brevity.

.

We don't let go. We live in. Absence. That irradiated, small road. And we will remember the signs.

NOTES

The text on page 29 is inspired by C.D. Wright's "Imaginary August."

"The Birth Manual" incorporates text from *The Complete Midwife's Practice Enlarged* (1697) by Thomas Chamberlayne.

The images on pages 34 and 35 are derived from William Smellie's *A Sett of Anatomical Tables, with Explanations, and an Abridgement, of the Practice of Midwifery* (1754), courtesy US National Library of Medicine.

The notion of the Midwest as "the desert of the real" is derived from "Modes of Digital Identification: Virtual Technologies and Webcam Cultures" by Ken Hillis, where he writes that "[i]f Wyoming and Nebraska are 'the heartland,' they are also battlegrounds—the deserts of the real."

The text on page 53 is inspired by Sylvia Plath's "The Detective."

The image on page 55 is derived from *Packing House and Cold Storage Construction; a General Reference Work on the Planning, Construction, and Equipment of Modern American Meat Packing Plants* (1915) by Hans Peter Henschien.

The text on page 56 is inspired by Daniel Borzutzky's *In the Murmurs of the Rotten Carcass Economy.*

The quotes in italics on pages 57-64, 68, and 70-80 are derived from "Blood, Sweat, and Fear: Workers' Rights in U.S. Meat and Poultry Plants" published by Human Rights Watch at https://www.hrw.org/reports/2005/usa0105/ and "Interviews with Mothers of Young Children in the SEED for Oklahoma Kids" published by the Center for Social Development at the George Warren Brown School of Social Work at https://csd.wustl.edu/publications/documents/rp12-53.pdf. Some quotes have been rearranged or slightly modified for sense and tense. In

Heartland TV: Prime Time Television and the Struggle for U.S. Identity, Victoria E. Johnson includes border states like Oklahoma in her definition of the heartland, and this book also takes a broader view of the region.

The text on page 65 is inspired by Ted Kooser's "Late February."

The text on page 81 references *A Child is Being Killed* by Carolyn Zaikowski.

ACKNOWLEDGEMENTS

Thank you to the editors of *Dream Pop Press*, where excerpts
from THE BONEYARD, THE BIRTH MANUAL, A BURIAL:
INVESTIGATIONS INTO THE HEARTLAND originally appeared.

Thank you to Emily Abrons, Rachel Bailin, Megan Burns, Steven Dunn,
Molly Faerber, Josh Fomon, Tony Flesher, Rebecca Franklin, Peter
Giebel, Jane Gregory, Brandi Homan, W. Scott Howard, Russell Jaffe,
Philip Kennedy, Meredith Luby, Caroline Manring, Mira Mos Crime,
Selah Saterstrom, Charles Shields, Eleni Sikelianos, Billy J. Stratton,
Sasha Strelitz, Adam Tedesco, C.D. Wright, my students, my family, and
Trembling Pillow Press for publishing this book.

Julia Madsen is a multimedia poet and educator. She received an MFA in Literary Arts from Brown University and is currently a PhD candidate in English/Creative Writing at the University of Denver. Her poems, multimedia work, and reviews have appeared in *jubilat, Black Warrior Review, Versal, Caketrain, Michigan Quarterly Review, Alice Blue Review, CutBank, La Vague Journal, Flag+Void, Word For/Word, Entropy, Fanzine, Tagvverk, Dream Pop Press,* and elsewhere.

Trembling Pillow Press

I of the Storm by Bill Lavender
Olympia Street by Michael Ford
Ethereal Avalanche by Gina Ferrara
Transfixion by Bill Lavender
Downtown by Lee Meitzen Grue
SONG OF PRAISE   Homage To John Coltrane by John Sinclair
DESERT JOURNAL by ruth weiss
Aesthesia Balderdash by Kim Vodicka
SUPER NATURAL by Tracey McTague
I LOVE THIS AMERICAN WAY OF LIFE by Brett Evans
Q by Bill Lavender
loaded arc by Laura Goldstein
Want for Lion by Paige Taggart
Trick Rider by Jen Tynes
May Apple Deep by Michael Sikkema
Gossamer Lid by Andrew Brezna
simple constructs for the lizzies by Lisa Cattrone
FILL: A Collection by Kate Schapira and Erika Howsare
Red of Split Water a burial rite by Lisa Donovan
CUNTRY by Kristin Sanders
Kids of the Black Hole by Marty Cain
Feelings by Lauren Ireland
If You Love Error So Love Zero by Stephanie Anderson
The Boneyard, The Birth Manual, A Burial: Investigations into the Heartland by Julia Madsen

Forthcoming Titles:

Unoriginal Danger by Dominique Salas
You've Got A Pretty Hellmouth by Michael Sikkema
HEAD by Christine Kanownik
Book of Levitatons by Anne Champion and Jenny Sadre-Orafai

Trembling Pillow Press

Bob Kaufman Book Prize

2012: *Of Love & Capital* by Christopher Rizzo (Bernadette Mayer, judge)

2013: *Psalms for Dogs and Sorcerers* by Jen Coleman (Dara Wier, judge)

2014: *Natural Subjets* by Divya Victor (Anselm Berrigan, judge)

2015: *there are boxes and there is wanting* by Tessa Micaela Landreau-Grasmuck (Laura Mullen, judge)

2016: *orogeny* by Irène Mathieu (Megan Kaminski, judge)

Made in the USA
San Bernardino, CA
17 January 2019